STILL FURTHER

POETRY

Occasional Light (Mantis Poets / David Philip, 1979)

I Live Here Now (LHA, 1979)

Hong Kong Portraits (Perpetua Press, 1986)

In the Water-Margins (Snailpress / Crane River, 1994)

Holiday Haiku (Snailpress, 1997)

Requiem (Belgrave Press, 1997)

So Far: Selected Poems, 1960–2004 (Snailpress / JCEL, 2005)

Citizen of Elsewhere: Selected Poems (Happenstance, 2013)

Before (Crane River / African Sun Press, 2018)

NOVELS

Elegy for a Revolutionary (Faber, 1969; Faber Finds, 2010)

Send War in Our Time, O Lord (Faber, 1970; Faber Finds, 2011)

Death of Fathers (Faber, 1972; Faber Finds, 2011)

A Messiah of the Last Days (Faber, 1974; Faber Finds, 2010)

Shades of Darkness (Jonathan Ball, 2004)

BIOGRAPHY AND MEMOIR

Patrick Duncan: South African and Pan-African (HEB, 1980; James Currey / David Philip, 2000)

My Brother & I (Kingston University Press, 2013)

Used to be Great Friends (Mampoer Shorts, 2013)

The Man with the Suitcase: The Life, Execution & Rehabilitation of John Harris, Liberal Terrorist (Crane River, 2015)

Some Schools (John Catt Educational, 2016)

VERSE FOR CHILDREN

Moose, Mouse and Other Rhymes (Peridot Press, 2011)

STILL FURTHER

NEW POEMS 2000–2020

BY

C.J. DRIVER

UHLANGA

2021

ACKNOWLEDGEMENTS

Most of these poems were written after the publication of *So Far: Selected Poems, 1960-2004*. Only three of the poems in the pamphlet, *Citizen of Elsewhere*, published by the Happenstance Press in 2013, are included here. 'A Sort of Prayer' was included in *A Book of Friends* in honour of JM Coetzee's 80th birthday. Others have been published in *New Contrast, Carapace, Times Literary Supplement*, the *Yale Review, Tears in the Fence, The Use of English, Oxford Poetry, The Oxford Magazine, Areté, Stanzas, Poetry Review, The Spectator* and *Baobab*. 'Telling the Truth' and 'Poem against Rain' were published first in *Branch-Lines: Edward Thomas and Contemporary Poetry* (ed. Guy Cuthbertson & Lucy Newlyn, Enitharmon Press, 2007). 'A Winter's Day at Westonbirt' was first published by the Forestry Commission in a newsletter.

Several of these poems were written while I held a Bogliasco Fellowship at the Liguria Study Centre for the Arts and Humanities in 2007, while I was a resident at the MacDowell Colony in New Hampshire in the autumn of 2009, and while I held a fellowship in the Hawthornden International Writers' Retreat in Scotland in 2013. I am grateful to the trustees and staff of all three places for giving me time and space away from other commitments. From 2007 I had the useful advantage of an honorary attachment to the School of Literature and Creative Writing at the University of East Anglia; I am especially grateful for the practical encouragement and critical good sense of Professor Jon Cook of that university, and for the help and friendship of those at the Writers' Centre in Norwich, especially Chris Gribble.

I acknowledge with thanks the help and advice given by various friends and relations, particularly my wife, Ann; my sister, Professor Dorothy Driver; JM Coetzee; my daughter, Tamlyn Ann Driver;

and the late and lamented Professor Dan Jacobson, for some years my first reader. Douglas Reid Skinner has been a friend for years but more recently has become more and more an invaluable editor, knowledgeable and meticulous. Maeder Osler, who appears in these poems in many guises, has been my closest friend for sixty years. I lean on his strength and wisdom.

I have been with the same literary agency, to my advantage but hardly theirs, since 1965, and am grateful to Andrew Hewson of that agency, now called Johnson & Alcock, for his loyal support over the years.

– C.J.D.

CONTENTS

In England Now
for Kate Wilson

*"I don't think you belong to any country
in particular when you are old."*

– *NIGEL BALCHIN,* Darkness Falls from the Air

Before the dawn, a dream of what I lost
By leaving when I did; and then the sky
   Blood-streaked enough for home, and I
      Remembered what you asked.

"But haven't you already made your choice?
You've lived in England more than half your life,
   You have a house, career, a wife –
      Even an English voice."

Old friend, you know quite well how much I've changed –
But still I need those deep horizons, where
   (With no impediment but air)
      The far-flung land is ranged.

You say I'm almost English now – should keep
Myself concealed? A fractured part of me,
   My heart perhaps, will always be
      In Africa: when I'm asleep

Or when the early breezes shift the haze
Of mornings into Sussex summer skies,
   The promises of heat revive
      Those distant dusty days.

So, if we "immigrants from overseas"
Have found in England rich security,
    Since here one may be almost free –
        "Such teeming destinies"

Once held in England's boundless "master-work"
Come now to sweep the streets, or teach, or nurse –
    Must we be told that we should curse
        Our past as wholly dark?

Accumulated anguish for a name
And nothing good to find, but grief in loads
    Piled up like cairns on mountain roads
        To fool an exile home?

And yet both here and there I'm tainted by the past –
An Englishman come lately back again,
    Who thought that he might skip the pain,
        Colonial to the last.

So here I stay, half-hoping still to go.
The claim of birth would be of little use
    If once again I made a choice.
        The years are not so slow.

The morning spreads its wings; the ash-tree leaves
Are making music out of light and shade;
    The early colours smudge and fade;
        A roosting ring-dove grieves.

I am in England now: old hypocrite,
Who bows and smiles and nods and does his best
To seem content. I'm loyal at least –
Or is this still deceit?

Cove Rock, Igoda River Mouth

The deconstructed triangles
  of seagulls' prints
    criss-cross the rippled sand.

The tide is sliding out
  as imperceptible as time:
    I do not count these days.

Sailors shipwrecked on this shore
  would walk for ever westwards:
    survival still surprises.

A long-necked cormorant appears
  and just as suddenly is gone.
    The sun comes slanting off the sea.

A fledgling gull as grey and white
  as breaking waves
    saunters on the debris' edge.

When Makana lost his tragic war,
  this is where he came to weep.
    His children's children wept much more.

The surf is cursing close at hand
  like history writ large:
    the wind says something else.

Where waves implode in hidden coves,
   ancestral voices boom
         like creatures of the deep, half-men, half-fish.

Though water makes for fluctuating reverie,
   the sand comes rifling down
         from finite edges of the dunes.

At the Grave of Cecil John Rhodes

Black eagles chart the upper air.
Elephant-shrews streak across the rock.

We've come to view an ancient grave.
This man owned the whole country once.

Our tour-guide, whose name is Lonely,
Tramps uphill with a crate of drinks.

We are his first tourists for weeks.
He has no time for Zimbabwe.

Politicians are (he says) locusts.
Who hoped to learn from history?

The sun goes down like a balloon.
The lichen will outlast us all.

Remembering Kashmir

On Lake Nageen, in Sultan Wangnoo's care:
the flower-sellers came in the morning,
paddling their boats through the water lilies
to peddle their wares for what seemed nothing
(and worth much to hear their English sales talk
learned by rote, and hardly comprehended,
though enchantingly chanted all the same)
and we leaned out of the houseboat's windows
into the scent of wallflowers, asters,
sword lilies, pinks, golden bells, hyacinths –
with the Shalimar Gardens across the lake.

Then, into the mountains, the high meadows
frozen still, but spring beginning to break.
Somewhere up above us lay Shangri-la,
so we imagined, as we trudged higher.
At fourteen thousand feet, the snow god struck me down,
fixed a band around my brain, then tightened it
until I couldn't see the path. We came down,
swiftly then, two days' walking done in one,
risking the ice bridges despite their melting.

Yet I remember Kashmir as paradise
as it might have been, as it once was
perhaps, before boundaries split the people
in half, before religion became
not what a man or woman might believe
but a sword to strike down the infidel,
or a bomb to toss into a crowded mosque,
though we pray to the same God for the same grace.

In the Lodi Garden, New Delhi

In the Lodi Garden
dark-eyed women saunter,
saris furled and folded,
voices clashing gaily.

In the Lodi Garden
tombs still shelter lovers,
shards of blue remaining,
laughter in the distance.

In the Lodi Garden
saddhus stride severely.
Shoals of scholars follow,
silently reforming.

In the Lodi Garden
runners lard the footpaths,
dodging past the walkers,
calling out rejoinders.

In the Lodi Garden
prophet, priest and fakir
share the failing daylight,
quietly conversing.

In the Lodi Garden
everything is sacred:
all we are, or have been,
gathered in this garden.

Misanthropic Sonnets from the Caribbean

I

Older now, but still as ignorant as sin
and knowing even less about so much,
my rationality has worn too thin
to be repaired, and gloom's my constant crutch.
I'm almost pleased to reach the end of days
and wear 'curmudgeon' as an honoured badge;
'foul-tempered git' is just as good as praise,
so balanced am I on the very edge.
I'll come at last, to my bemused surprise,
to where I started from, a mewling child
encased in diapers, who cries and cries,
"Nurse, nurse, I need the pan." By age defiled,
I shall not care; I'll smile and let it go.
Is that my nasty smell? I wouldn't know.

Did I say 'diapers'? Seems that Trinidad
has got to me quite soon. Kiskadee birds
to add 'confu'? 'Soca' to drive me mad?
Piarco Airport mutter mumble words
indecipherable? In Tobago,
a brown man shouted, "No one understan'
what you tryin' to say," which helped me know
it wasn't only me "wid de problem, man".
There's nothing racial saying noise is 'white' –
it's what I hear, again, again: every speech
except the one I think I want. The night
at Thy command comes...? This the pitch we reach
when all else fades? When thunder from the reef
is softer than the falling of a leaf?

A crossroads and a broken traffic light:
a tourist stranded in a jam, I sign
(my palm upturned, so English, so polite)
a car to squeeze ahead into the line.
The driver winds his window down and yells
abuse. Nonplussed, I smile and try to wave
to signal peace – but get more "shit" and "balls"
and "cunt", until the queue begins to move.
That sign (my son explains with half a smile)
means something else. You could have got much worse
than rage; he might quite well have had some steel.
You got off very lightly with a curse.
This isn't home, old man: it's Trinidad.
You take it as it is, both good and bad.

4

With age comes irresponsibility:
a pleasant thing to be removed from all
that once controlled (so acquiescingly)
what I had thought would last. For curtain call,
there comes not the silence that I feared
but garrulity – a need to buttonhole
an absent audience with tales once heard
too many years ago. Upon my soul,
my dears, here's something that I'm sure you'll want
to hear, the gist of which you're bound to get
if you're prepared to wait. Enlarge the font
to fourteen point; do not adjust the set;
the priest will signal when it's time to grieve;
the exit signs will show you how to leave.

5

A sudden tropic rain, as uncontrolled as rage,
but still the heat does not abate. The frogs
are screaming in the ditch. Why should old age
be so undignified? The builders' dogs
come barking out, as if to chase off tramps:
"Get off, you scum, you mongrel curs," I shout
and wave my stick. "They'd never bite old Gramps,"
the workman says, as if he's found me out.
"You Yank?" he asks. "No, English," I reply –
or should I tell him what I really am?
Is it a kind of scorn to tell a lie
so small, in fact? Vociferous I am,
except about the bits that matter most:
here's nothing to unwrap my screwed-up past.

At the End of the Day
(at the Liguria Study Centre, Bogliasco)

The sun comes sliding off the sea
to filch the gleams
from glass that tops the villa walls.
A mixed quartet is tuning up,
down the road: fiddles, cello, horn – and brakes.
Women call and men reply. You'd think
that they were arguing if they didn't laugh.
Subito and sub-terra sings the train.

Pitched out to catch the light, the pines
loom above the terraced paths. The cars
go crunching down a gravel drive,
marcato, where some days – or weeks – ago
a gardener tidied needles into heaps.
The waves are talking to the shore
while gulls scream haphazardly.

Sostenuto calls the dove
from where the cornice fell last year.
A boy has painted something rude
on lucid stone.
A builder's skip has blocked a passageway;
the paint is peeling, façade fades, iron flakes,
the cobblestones are loosened in the road
and (rallentando) down the buildings fall.

And yet a hint of jasmine scents the air;
the trees are sequenced orange, lemon, lime.
The dog – whose name's Allegro – hunts a squirrel
in the dried-up grass.
The order of the day is lento, lento
diminuendo. There's something
on the very edge of what I want to say.
The sun is dropping down below the sea.
It has to do with quiet ways to end.
      Like this.

Orchard Cottage

White wisteria
over an old oak door:
snowfall in midsummer.

Poem Against Rain

All day I have been walking. My view
of the small part of England that's mine
has been rained away. There's nothing
that belongs to me in this rotting place,

no house, no memory – even my body
is losing its battle with age, stumbles
in the slack fat and the hard breathing
for the comfort of home. It is raining

also the slow collapse of the hills,
and no thunder in the sky or the clay;
and my head is falling too slowly down
for my curses to break this coward,

my body, small feeble brother flesh,
of his clinging to the closed sky's hand.
The rain marches before. I have lost
all day my private war with the rain.

A Winter's Day at Westonbirt

A storm smashed through the park
last night. The branches torn from evergreens
are littered on the paths and lawns,
and tractors' deepest ruts are filled brimful.
An ancient oak is fenced for safety's sake
with branches opened wide as arms;
it stood upright throughout the gale
as if it knew by now how not to fall.

So, think about this place in England now,
think about this arboretum, made to show
a rich man's large and generous grasp
of how his world had changed and grown,
that godly range of goodly things
that England thought it made secure.
Think about this country now, its empire gone,
still sure that all it gave was always good.

The names alone might make a poem:
whitebeam, wild cherry, wych elm, maple, yew,
spruce, magnolia, rowan, silver birch,
alder, chestnut, ash, hawthorn, box, bay, lime,
scattered, gathered, lined in avenues
or grouped in magic rings,
surprising in their symmetry
or seeming random in the way they've spread.

Of all the trees I prize the most,
cedar must be first: foreign import (yes!)
and apt to spiral out of shape
for all the praise inspired in Lebanon,
but stubborn, strong and awkward as it twists
and spreads, and wider spreads
for every year, despite the scars
of winter gales and summer dereliction.

Too cold, today, for pausing much to stare
at rarities or speculate on heights;
but still the sightlines open out as planned
for landscapes trapped as if in convex glass.
A family goes past, in boots and coats
and scarves and gloves, the elderly in front,
determined on their Sunday exercise,
their children holding back, complaining hard:

"We want our tea..." "Can't we go home?"
"I'm bored with trees..." Our own are playing tag,
or weaving down the avenue of limes,
or finding cones like custard cups
to let their parents hold in store for them.
Each little gang has stopped to stare
at what the other sees as strange.
There's no attempt to fraternise.

The storm is coming back tonight,
or so the forecast claims: is England
well prepared? There's grim self-satisfaction here
in coping with disaster: we do it well
or so our people like to think.
Although we groan and whine, and whinge and moan,
we think that in the end we'll stand as one,
while other nations fall apart.

For storms are nothing new; and empires end,
or systems fail, the old die off,
the young renew. So, seedlings root,
so saplings shoot, so oak is anchored deep
and shallow beech capsized.
The rhododendron turns again to ponticum
and spreads like weed, and no one knows
how tall these English Wellingtonia grow.

Another gang of kids goes laughing past,
their hoods pulled up to hide their heads –
one idly throws an empty can away,
another drops her half-smoked cigarette.
I puzzle what they think they're doing here –
these lawless, noisy, adolescent louts –
till one commands the others to admire
viburnum's early blossoming.

For this is England now:
a complicated place, both rich and poor,
hemmed in with silly rules which most obey –
but passionately free. Who else would share
such space without regard to ownership?
Or who would dump their litter from a car
as they were on the road to Westonbirt?
Who now would plant three thousand different trees?

Here's one with branches tangled like a maze –
that's ironwood, and this is juniper,
and that a tulip tree, with lantern fruit
arranged between the four-lobed leaves.
A whitebeam with its silver bark and buds
directs our way.
We've circled round the paths, and find ourselves
precisely where we were before.

A chunk of time itself is gathered here,
upended like a stone to mark the road
from where we were to where we are,
not just a relic of a rich man's pride:
this is a breathing space for England,
in time as well as place,
a pause between the empire that was lost
and where we're going next, which no one knows.

Winter Song in the Karoo

The cold came hurtling down from the north,
bending all before in its headlong path,
    ripping awns from the love-grass,
        pounding eaves of the farmhouse.

The sunset sailed in the wake of the cold,
crimson, orange and grey, spangled with gold,
    shaping the clouds to the land,
        etching their shadows in sand.

The daylight lapsed as sudden as thunder
emptying twilight out of the window;
    the nighttime gathered like sheep
        and darkness fell into sleep.

I looked at my face in the midnight glass
but forgot who I'd been, where I was:
    old, and distraught with despair,
        counting down time, adding up fear.

The ring-doves are weeping at the hayloft door,
crystals of frost patterned on the bathroom floor:
    I am trapped in an old desire,
        grievously burned in that cold fire.

Lawn-sprinklers left turning throughout the night
are fixed in fountains of ice, pillars of light:
    droplets now frozen to lace
        finish this song with timely grace.

Sea Fret

The sea fret falls without a word
on the lone fisherman
and the couple out for a walk.

The plaint of the oystercatchers
comes before we see them
low-flying into our vision.

This is more than mist, less than rain:
we brush droplets away
from eyebrows, forearms and t-shirts.

Half a mile down the beach, sunshine –
and half a mile inland:
here, we test the invisible.

Beyond the shark's-tooth ridge of rock
we can still hear breakers;
the sea oils into the pools.

The way we came has been closed down.
only the water's edge
tells us the way home.

Small Town, Old Age

i.m. Phyllis Baines (neé Driver) and Capel Baines

1

The sound of old people talking
in a small kitchen,
amiably sharing their work:
like the constant cooing of doves:
To-to-rue-to, to-to-rue-to;
To-to-to-rue, to-to-to-rue.

2

Here in the garden's dappled shade –
or perhaps it's dappled sunlight;
or, overhead, a dappling tree.

3

Lemon tree, lemon tree,
green and yellow, yellowy-green
just edging its way to yellow.

4

Angry voices on a pavement,
a dog grumbling behind a gate,
a car alarm going off for no reason,
a baby crying as if she meant it,
a bang sounding like a gunshot:
a door opens somewhere briefly
and noises that might be music
come screaming from a radio.

5

In the patio a plum tree spreads itself
so ample in its harvest we cannot catch
all that falls from sunlight to shade;
so we find ourselves in the end cursing
the soggy fruit as it tumbles to stain
shirts, tablecloths, and all that it touches.

6

A sliver of moon, sliced as thin
as cucumber for a sandwich,
translucent as a kaleidoscope
and in colour somewhere between
pink and yellow, with wisps of white.

7

The hadada wakes us; later says
it's time to go home. The boubou shrike
is hiding in the dark. Swallows
converse in air. The coucal makes a noise
like water falling in a mountain stream.

8

As an old bricklayer peers at a wall
to exclaim that whoever did that job
knew what he was up to, all right I tell you –
not what you see now, just slapped down
in a hurry, with no feeling for brick,
no sense of pattern or design, or how
things ought to be, because they ought, you see:

so we might say this is how we should live,
in our own space, quiet, with a garden
and fruit trees, a few flowers, and neighbours
who will not mind us, but will mind for us
as we get older, needing order,
and things arranged as they ought to be.
We stand at the gate, looking out, dismayed.

9

Old age presses in on us like a crowd
of strangers with accents and hairstyles,
some of them pierced with ornaments.
I'm sure they don't mean to be threatening
as they jostle us along the pavements:
we have had our day,
but we must have lost it somewhere.

10

I had forgotten the colour of cannas –
which are not just red, but gold as well,
and shades between, vermilion, crimson,
ochre even: flame coloured – and below,
maroon tinged with blue... wildly various.

Someone

I thought I saw someone in the hall
in the far corner of my eye
as we sat late after dinner:

a man (I thought it was) in a suit,
dark grey, I saw – or maybe black –
crossing the cones of my sight.

Not there, of course, when I went to look –
left the table to search, mark you,
bravely opening doors to the dark.

Was it the wine, not talking but seeing?
That last glass before we rose
to amble into the garden?

But I was almost sure I'd seen him
and I think I heard a door shut
gently, like a page being turned,

and did I smell the slightest whiff
of aftershave – sandalwood perhaps
but branded with a hint of hell.

A Song for Sighing

Oh, this is a song for sighing,
a song for the years we have missed,
a song to add to our praying,
to shore up the past when it's lost.

Oh, this is a song for parting,
a song as we go on our way,
a small regret in our doubting,
heart-starved and wondering why.

This is a song for the friends we lost,
drifting apart or running away,
a song for the things that didn't last
but that seemed so fine on the day.

Oh, this is a song for leaving,
a way of waving goodbye,
a glance at the loss of our loving
or a shrug in accepting a lie.

Oh, this is a song for the dancers
side-stepping the risks we survived,
a tribute paid to the chancers
by whose failings others were saved.

Oh, this is a song for the ending,
as the planets and stars expand,
as the meaning itself is changing
and the sea re-covers the land.

The Security Policeman's Song

Ag, man, I'm very sorry now
about what happened then –
just what we need not say, all right?
Not why, nor where, nor when.

Jus' a job I had to do, my friend,
like any other one;
and now we're mainly reconciled:
what's done is surely done.

It's orders that the law gave out,
it's orders I obeyed:
I did the things that I was told
to earn what I was paid.

I took no pleasure in the work,
I didn't strut about.
I took my place behind the crowd
and got my notebook out.

And now I sit here on the stoep
and rock my chair just so:
my pension comes in like a charm
and still my savings grow.

I wouldn't call it truth, my friend,
I wouldn't call it lies.
It's politics that comes and goes –
jus' try that out for size.

And you, my friend, are somewhere else,
and rising still so fast.
I trust you won't remember now
that time I saw you last.

We have a kind of friendship now,
the gaolers and the gaoled:
I'm me, and you are you, all right –
who knows which one has failed?

I won't presume to wave my hand
to say, "Hullo, my friend":
I may just gravely nod my head
to signify the end.

The Hymn of the Christian Atheist

If scoffers ask if I believe
That stuff about a virgin birth,
That water's wine, or wine transmutes,
That God took flesh and came to earth,
    I say I have my doubts.

And yet I always go to church.
I know the hymns by heart, I say
The creed, I chant the psalms, I read
The lessons when I'm asked. I pray
    As if I thought God heard.

I note the vicar's kindly voice
Explaining what the scriptures meant.
I nod at learned points made well;
I even give things up for Lent,
    Though what I never tell.

I stand, I sit, I kneel, I take
The bread and dip it in the wine.
I see the candles gutter in the wind
But never take it as a sign
    It was because I sinned.

And when the begging bowl comes round,
I always put in rather more
(Of course with details for Gift Aid)
Than I would do if I were poor
    And not, thank God, well paid.

I'm friendly to the others there,
But none too keen to shake the hand
Of someone I don't know. 'The Peace'
Enrages me; I'd like it banned –
    I treat it like a curse.

If angels ever sang to me,
I fear I didn't hear. I lack
The magic that would mean belief.
My path is lonely, slow and bleak
    And strewn, I guess, with grief.

I'm fairly sure there is no God.
The reason that I always go
Is not for fear I may be wrong;
For if I am, I'll surely know
    Before too very long.

Substitute Trophy Head

(Object No.153, Sainsbury Collection, University of East Anglia)

I stare at the world
through the slits of my cowrie eyes.

Paint whitens my scars
to simulate weeping.

I am not death but a substitute,
not the real thing, not even a trophy.

I was never a man; I merely pretended.
My grin was always upside down.

I am neither victim nor victor.
I am the stump of a tree in no man's land.

I am the silence that comes after Alas,
the one voice that never says Amen.

I have seen everything.
It is not good.

Regression

When everything is said and done,
Each item on his list ticked off,
The chairman taps the desk to say,
"We don't know when we'll meet again."

Between the action and its end,
One tries to find necessity,
Precisely what it seems to be,
"And don't forget the way it was."

Between the thought and action came
A shiver that I can't explain.
It might be that some stranger said:
"It wouldn't be the proper thing to do."

Before the thought there came a pause
As if to urge delay. The book
Fell open at a page that said:
"A reassessment might be wise."

Before the pause there was a night
When fear had not yet learned its name:
The child still begged they leave a light
"And please don't close the bedroom door."

Before the age when things joined up
And days and days became a week,
He learned that love had gone away
And crying didn't bring it back.

A Lamentation

Now that she's old and invisible,
she stares frankly at the Bright Young Things
prancing on pavements, posing in trains
and they barely notice her looking –
  she's as useless as experience.

Once there's no one nearby who knows her,
she finds herself a place on the steps
and sits there, in the sun, pretending
she's waiting for someone to meet her –
  she's as patient as sleeping policemen.

No one cares anymore she's grumpy;
she whinges; they don't even listen –
"Who's that old moaner in the raincoat?"
They mutter as they wander away –
  inconsequential as argument.

Was that the chair that creaked as she rose?
Is it the floor that tilts as she walks?
Who was it waving from the window?
Where are her glasses, where is her book?
  So what if she sleeps through the programme?

When the postman comes (usually late),
she consigns the letters addressed to her
post-haste to the wastepaper basket
because she's sure they aren't hers really;
    she's as cynical as circulars.

Persuaded by pain there's something wrong,
she takes her place in the doctor's queue,
but, by the time she gets to see him,
she can't remember where the pain was –
    she's as forgetful as flowers.

Now that she's old and invisible
she doesn't recall quite what it was like
when people could see her. She stumbles
on broken pavements into the dark –
    visible only in alleyways.

Neighbours

Eros has gone to live somewhere nearby
but I seem to have mislaid his address.
Thanatos has now moved into the house:
I see him hobbling about the garden –
leaning on his stick to pluck the deadheads,
sniffing blooms, then wincing as he straightens.
Later, I notice him in a deckchair
fast asleep, with his face getting sunburned
so that his hair seems even more sparsely white.
He talked to me yesterday at great length,
leaning forward confidentially
on the garden gate. His breath is bad.
Still, in some ways, he is like an old friend.
I prefer him to that cocksure upstart.

Song for an Unborn Brother

The one who should have been the first,
my mother lost at thirteen weeks.
My parents saved his name for me
and one there sleeps, and one here wakes.

I wonder what he might have been
since what I am would not exist.
What little gap there seems to be
between my body and the dust.

So when I'm dead (as dead as him)
will I then seem as never born?
A shadow lost when lights went out?
A match head struck that didn't burn?

Abundance thrives despite our loss:
the glass reflects, the glass refracts –
my brother's flesh and my own self
still suppositions more than facts.

Simple Song
i.m. Ingrid Jonker

Star-crossed, says the night;
word-cursed, says the day:
piecemeal, patchwork;
matchwood, password.

Faithless, says the boy;
heartless, says the girl:
lovelorn, hopeless;
fearsome, far-flung.

Heartsore, says the head;
headstrong, says the heart:
head start, heartache;
heartbreak, headlong.

Makeweight, says the wind;
feckless, says the sun:
windswept, woeful;
far gone, fare well.

Conversation in the Bushveld

Here I am again, in late middle age
(or is this early old age?) carrying
a rifle "weighing little more than a small dog
and costing about the same as a chicken",
in self-defence, against a stray lion
or a herd of buffalo, the old chaps
patrolling the near edge of the herd,
tilting their nostrils upwards to make sure
we are no threat – as I seldom am, these days,
always on the edge of things now, myself,
old warhorse, centaur if you're feeling kind,
having devoted my years to teaching...

This is a gun. If you point it at someone
and pull this lever – we call it a trigger –
the person falls down. Just like that. Dead,
usually. But if they're not dead, you point it
again, closer, and you pull. Then they're dead.

When they're dead, they don't know who you are.
They probably didn't beforehand, either,
Unless they were someone in your family.
You must do this when we tell you, and then
we'll be very pleased with you, like in school.
I tell you, there are no such things as ghosts.

...Are they the same children who are driven now,
laughing, through minefields towards machine guns?
Are they high on something? Are they paying
back what we bought them for, years ago?
Before they were born, even? Too easy
to say we have no answers: we had
the questions in the first place. What did it cost
to come to this? What shall we have to pay
before we turn our well-worn rifles over
to ancient authorities? They weigh nothing now;
children aim them better than their elders.

Footnote for an Autobiography

"You do realise," said my professor
forty-two years ago) "this will mean no work
ever" in what were called then 'government' schools.
Well, that state fell, though by then I was stateless
essentially, though I guarded my passport.
Amazing it happened at all, that exit
from what had seemed a suicidal fortress:
the grim-faced custodians stood aside
from the barricades where they might have stayed to fight –
and not before time, though still surprising.
I had already chosen otherwise.
Small mercies mount up as one gets older;
pension accumulates, savings aren't spent,
kindly concern counts more than passion
and rage is mainly a lack of dignity.
I am no longer, thank God, a teacher.
If you learn from me, it is by default.
Look at what I do, then do otherwise.

Au Contraire
After reading Ovid's Black Sea Letters

Reverse exile, then, to be sent to London from the provinces –
except that I loathed London with its cliques and claques, chattering hacks,
scratching of backs, puffing of books by friends and fawning favourites
("This most worthy successor to his already distinguished work...")
or the putting down of an enemy ("the least said the better" –
meaning, "I couldn't even be bothered to read it through just once")
and the pretend voices, the glottal stops striving to swallow
evidence of middle-class upbringing in suburban households,
as if where we come from is shameful – and the elevation
of the cockeyed and crazy into a credo, as if madness
were the only sane response to a lunatic society –
and yet the point of conversation seemed to be the exclusion
of all but the circling few who knew the nicknames, schools and foibles
of everyone who could possibly be worth knowing –
or if I mentioned Kipling in their company, I was made
to feel I was just another rather stupid colonial –
or like the time, in an Oxford seminar, I compared Wordsworth
and Ginsberg, to try to show how poets use repetition...
You'd have thought I'd not washed for weeks, nor changed my shirt
  and underpants –
as when I dared suggest that if schooling were seen as privilege
rather than right, it might be taken just a jot more seriously...

Well, old friend, that's when I would think of you, back home, trapped
    on your farm,
refused a passport, banned to a single district, in detention
whenever the Special Branch fancied a bit of persecution,
surrounded by the Zulu "barbarians" whose language you spoke
"Like a native", and who honoured you – though a white man – like
    a chief;
it was you whom I most admired, whom I would have liked to parade
in a London gathering where "liberal" was a term of abuse –
and you would have smiled, found a beer, punctured pretence with
    a sentence,
and cooled me down with slow questions, local details and brooding facts;
no wonder so many leaned on you in those "years of oppression",
the nightmare years when we thought the only exit would be bloodshed,
though knew that the weak and innocent go down in front of the tanks
before they reach their targets. You survived, and there was no honour,
except among friends: "lib'ral" (spit it out!) is still pejorative...

Extracts from a Diary

"From lightning & tempest; from earthquake, fire & flood;
from plague, pestilence & famine; from battle & murder,
and from sudden death, Good Lord, deliver us."
– The Book of Common Prayer

Important to note, finally, that we require
not saving from death, but from "sudden death":
the other kind we may at best postpone...

But the waiting isn't easy. The multitudinous dead crowd us,
all shapes and sizes, all those old friends gone walkabout,
pushing their way into the carriage, looking for handholds...

And sometimes one thinks, "How lucky I am. He's younger than me,"
then wonders, "But why haven't I been chosen?
Is there something worse in wait for me, than a quick and quiet
    departure?"

Something almost elegant, maybe, to die while out fishing
on a salmon stream in Scotland: to fold one's rod, pack one's creel,
put one's back against a pine tree, and wait for the ghillie –

or failing to wake from a snooze after lunch on a Saturday,
with the rugby on the sports channel, and the newspaper folded,
a cup of tea gradually getting cold on the table.

I write these careful fragments sitting in an armchair, next to my bed
in the wing of a hospital named after royalty.
Above me, the saline drip sits, saving my life (though it reminds me of
    a vulture)

and the notice at the end of the bed
("Whither, as to the bed's-feet, life is shrunke...")
has its stark instruction: "Nil by mouth".

The obituaries will tell those who read them a few partial truths
(What's the difference between a partial truth and a total lie?)
and the stonemason will copy the Latin he can't understand...

But who cares now, when the priest presses the button under his lectern,
the part-time organist misses a few more of the notes
and the curtains open with a brief view of the netherworld...

I have had a short stroll through the valley of the shadow of death.
The full tour will begin later.

Walking Along New Road

Another evanescent day:
the coppiced ash, uncut too long, has grown
helter-skelter sideways
as random as dandelions blown awry.
My desire is to get away
from obligation.

As raptors quarter fields, so I patrol
my illness. Pain may mean I don't know what:
a cancer grown, a copious bleed,
an injury neglected once upon a time.
The doctor says he thinks he knows.

I should no longer care.
You'd think by now I would have learned
at least a thing or two. To live
in utter ignorance might seem a boon –
so might faith, I guess,
with sure salvation promised on the other side.
As far as I can tell,
it's merely that the boatman wants his fare.
I'm sort of halfway there.

Is this the place I want to be?
Is this precisely what I need to know?
I'll walk an hour today,
avoiding hills.
The pulse rate whacks away
at ninety-nine,
and I must pause
for breath.
I used to run this route each second day,
then add a hill, or sprint, or extra mile.
I pause to count the lines the plough has made
across the field below the road.

Falling at the Last

For Christopher & Georgie Wates

The autumn sun comes slanting through the hedge
As if a sideways slouch might hide intent;
We're bound for darkness, tilting on the edge...

And somehow, knowing what it was one meant
To do or be, this seems a perfect time
To make a change. The trouble is one can't –

Unless one swigs a double slug of shame:
One's made so many promises, and now
Must stick to them, or else must scratch one's name.

It's not as if the race went on, round and round,
With marshals standing there, disconsolate.
It's not the sort of thing one had in mind

When one sat, grinning, at the starting gate.
We're heading for the fence, and then the sprint –
Not very far. So: time to hesitate,

Or else to veer across the rails, hell-bent
On self-destruction, or to canter off,
Along a grassy ride, whistling, insouciant.

Of course one gives a damn, but best to laugh
And tell the tales. He hitched a lift to Greece.
He joined the Foreign Legion. He cured his cough

In Tenerife. They set up shop in Nice.
He put his fiddle on his back and strolled
To Spain. He joined the Mounted Police...

The trouble is to find oneself grown old
And not to know. It's time to act your age,
Old alter ego says: where you have failed,

Accept your fate. Relax. No point in rage.
Be cool. Retreat. O Keeper of the Debt,
O Judge of all the world, O Holy Sage,

Whose side d'you take? The Kindly Ones forget
Their rules and smile. Things have gone awry.
There are many fallers – and the favourite

Dislodged his mount; distrait, distraught, astray,
The riderless are streaming for the fence.
Do we declare sufficient for the day

Or risk our winnings on a second chance?

Turtle

"We've told the authorities," a kind man says
when we take the dogs to investigate.
What kind of authority should one consult
about an old sea-creature, stranded, dying –
it would seem from its immobility –
on the edge of steep surf, in Florida?
The dogs sniff, paw, retreat; the waves wash
and the sand laps the encumbered, crusted shell.
I don't suppose there's much more we can do.
What kind of wisdom brings one to this shore?

Sunset & After

The tide is out, the sand is firm beneath
my feet, the sun about to set. I'm here
again on Noordhoek Beach. Another day
is sauntering to its casual end.
I've journeyed back from where I don't belong
to where I also don't belong. You'd think
so bright a sun might set the sea alight
as it comes tumbling down, engorged with flame;
instead its incandescence swiftly drowns.
Across the bay the lighthouse spaces out
an intermittent pulse: five, then four,
then seventeen, I count the seconds down
and wonder if I've got them right. It's not
as if I've lost my way and need a guide
to get me back. As darkness gains a hold,
the horses on their evening exercise
chase themselves from dune to vlei, lagoon
to dune again, then to the water's edge.
How dark the sea becomes. No novice rides
these waves, which twist and churn and double back,
then whiplash down, enough to break the spine
of someone insufficiently prepared.
The point of being here is not revealed;
perhaps you'd find it out from time to time
and wander on, pretending that you had
a plan. Not true, as far as I'm concerned.
If God has worked His purpose out, He's not told me.

The sun is bound to rise again, I'm sure,
although I may be far away. The tide
will wash away the prints and someone else
will walk this beach to watch the setting sun.
Will I be back again? There's no one knows.

In Kirstenbosch Gardens

Juffertjie-roer-in-die-nag

I stoop to read the name:
a grey-leafed bush sans bloom,
no shape, nor smell, nor show.
I mutter as I go,
"A puritan of plants:
who'd guess what this one wants?"

For, come the night, her scent
roams everywhere, intent
on catching all she can.
With profligate élan
she giggles as she sins,
completes what she begins:

O lovers come to me,
O close your eyes to see,
O bruise your lips on mine
and shiver as I shine.
I pay what no one owes,
I reap what no one sows.
So, turn again to see
what passion needs to be
and write it in your book:
old man, you have to look...
At dawn she's in her place
restored to grace,
demure,
obscure.

Bypass

I had always hoped that death might come up
facing forward, full-frontal, fat fucker,
big bastard, take him on or be taken
out, and how do you like that, Mister Death?

And he comes up from an alley, sneaking,
snaking, squirming on his belly, mongrel
death, hardly snarling, and I tell myself
watch that upwards-cheating, sudden bite.

And it's not me, that's the trouble. I thought
I'd be the one with boots on, unafraid
as the lions stalked into the forum:
there's nothing but to die with dignity.

Yet here I sit in the high gallery,
watching, with hands folded across my chest,
and there's nothing, nothing now to be done
except to wait, and then wait some more.

A Sunday in Ordinary Time

The month and year escape me now; but it was,
for sure, Sunday, and in ordinary time.
We were travelling, in France, going southwards
slowly, stopping when we saw somewhere special –
a safe place to swim under old sandstone cliffs,
a roadside glade with tables, or a café
in a car-free square with shade trees and awnings,
old men playing boules, concentrating loudly,
though pausing to shake new hands or to embrace
old friends. I'm never very good (I admit)
at stopping without any reason – like dusk,
or a grandchild who's crying in the back seat.
Our destination always drives me further;
but that Sunday I was for once careless –
content to listen, then look. And so we came
down a small road to the side of a river
where the bank opened out to grass and gravel,
a pattern of plane trees and picnic tables.
The river flowed broad and slow, as expansive
as experience, though with sudden eddies.
This is a good place for a feast, said my wife.

Across the river, barracks – police, I guessed –
squat and sombre, fenced against the passing road
but not the river. And from this block there came
to the grassy riverbank on the far side
as we were parking our car under the trees
three women bringing tables, chairs, tablecloths

and glasses, cold boxes, bottles, cutlery,
plates and covered dishes, a big black saucepan –
and then a brood of children, one in a pram,
one in a Moses basket sturdy enough
to have floated safely down the slow river,
then boys on their bikes, and girls with their hair down –
a dozen of them, I thought, though their moving
made it hard to be certain; summoned, they sat,
and I could count: twenty, including babies.

I did wonder where the men were, in that crowd
of families – police, on duty in a city,
or guarding football matches, or just absent
as fathers these days so often seem to be,
but it didn't matter on that strange Sunday
as we watched the feast on the opposite bank
and ate our own small fare, substantial enough
by our standards (a baguette, two cheeses, wine,
saucisson and nectarines), frugal by theirs
as we marvelled at the dishes carried out
to the riverbank; and all the children ate
as starvelings might, even babies fed spoonfuls
by their mothers and sisters – or were these aunts? –
till we wondered the riverbank didn't break
under the extra weight of all that feasting
to float flamboyantly downstream like a loosened buoy
or pleasure boat that has lost its anchorage.

Long before the feast was finished, we had gone,
replete ourselves, sleepily heading southwards –
and for all we know they could still be feasting
on a riverbank, in France, on a Sunday
extraordinary in ordinary time.

A Version of a Montale Poem
from Cuttlefish Bones

To sit at noon in dappled shade,
One's back against a wall,
To hear a blackbird scold a snake
With sudden chinking call;

To see a double file of ants
Go marching down a track
And then to lift one's eyes to where
A mountain bares its back.

To hear through pines the muffled sea
Rehearse an old refrain,
Cicadas shriek their monotone
Again, again, again.

One ventures back into the glare
To find there's still no peace:
The wall that seemed to prop one's rest
Is topped with broken glass.

The Writing on the Wall

Above us on the terraces the vines
  Are yellow leaved, picked clean,
And, higher still, the autumnal Apennines
  Are edged with mossy green.

Umbrella pines are leaning out to light
  Across the paths that climb and climb
In stone-ribbed steps. The summit's out of sight,
  The ending out of time.

I've always dreamed of going home again
  To where the green and gold combine,
So sure that getting back would help me gain
  My place in that design.

Instead, my little broken history
  Has left me far too much inclined
To value all that makes me think I'm free –
  Or scared at what I'd find.

So now above this pastel-coloured town
    That looks as if it grew from clay,
I wait to watch the sun go calmly down
        On yet another day

And where horizon curves a blur of blue
    And rosy pink as if a light
Has got itself entrapped within the view
        Before it turned to night

Or as an artist's careless thumb might smear
    Decisions once so finely made
They merely seem like guesswork now. It's here
        My constant claim must fade:

For if we didn't have a debt to time,
    If light like flowers didn't fall,
If stairs were not an ever upward climb,
        We wouldn't know at all

The little we're allowed to learn. The bells
    Of all the churches sound, resound,
Rebound off granite cliffs and marbled walls,
        And circle, circle round.

Should we like children learn to be content
    At last – at least – with what we've got?
That easy answer isn't what I meant
        At all, for I am not.

The brushstroke of an errant cypress bough,
　　As if by chance precisely there,
Defines the landscape as we see it now.
　　　　The choice is not despair

Or hope: it's work, and work, and no escape.
　　The olive-trees are bound in stone
But bend and twist to find a final shape
　　　　And every one its own.

An Interruption

i.m. Julia Swindells (1951–2011)

Depression did its worst. We might have guessed
that, when this world became a wood
where tigers roam, retreating good
would find itself entrapped by bad. The rest

we know too well. What else is there to say?
The printer's jammed, the ink's run dry?
Our kind may mourn, but never cry?
 In Yorkshire, understatement rules the day?

Her hands are poised above the piano keys;
it seems she can't decide which piece
to play. She turns to pull a face;
an eyebrow lifts as if she wants to quiz

an audience no longer there. We've gone
from her as she has gone from us;
and is this absence nothingness?
                        What's done is done

and all the poems we'd hoped that we might hear
are trapped between 'delete' and 'pause'.
They circle in the air like crows
disturbed by walkers on an upland moor.

Vergelegen
for Maeder Osler

A painter's eye might catch this light:
Retreating shades of purple, blue and grey,
Though grass that wind has stripped and whipped away
        Is brushstroked almost white.

The ostrich pace the boundary fence:
The mountains that we see so far away
Lie closer than our feeble senses say –
        Their distance mere pretence.

The call of cranes on close patrol
Comes rolling, rolling from the far-off plain
And downward stoop the falcons to maintain
        Horizons in control.

Korhaans crank upward into flight,
Then croak portentous warnings, storms of rain;
The clapper larks go flapping up, again,
        Then whistle down from sight.

Now in your fingers bruise a spray
Of pungent, half-dead leaves. Scent stains the air
And won't let go. Delight is always there –
        It dances, night and day.

Yet no one calls this place his own:
The fragile spirits of the dead peer out
From where they shelter on the level height
        To strike a sounding stone.

Their past disclaims both time and place:
Though knowledge gained by loss is hard to bear,
You've found just how it is to look despair
        Unflinching in the face.

This jade-clear light brings skies so near –
The stars and planets gathered in a crowd –
You'd think that if you were to call out loud
        They'd hear your voice up there.

Too late, too late to pray?
You smile, and say we have to learn to cope
With no more hope, not even hope of hope.
        It lies too far away.

Late Lesson

She likes the edge of gardens best,
where wilderness comes sidling in
like pupils late to class. Her eyes
are drawn to where the gaps in walls
allow a view of burnished fields
in summer blaze, and then the dark
where meadows meet the upland pines.

Below the hedge the weeds sneak back
to stretch their tendrils out, and catch
to climb and climb, evading blades
by twisting in, the lighter greens
of beech entwined with ivy leaves.
The paths are wrapped in dappled light
by tangled stuff the strimmer missed.

The judgments that she used to make
(so profligate) – "a clever girl",
"a naughty boy" (the sort she liked
though never said) – have disappeared
like end-of-season daffodils;
their names are with her still, though now
no longer tied to how they looked.

Jack-by-the-hedge, and lady's smock,
or old man's beard and briar rose,
all things that should have been expelled,
come creeping, creeping back; and thus
a garden turns to what it was:
"I learned too late to let things be,"
she sighs to fields that flow away.

Song for the Grandchildren

A summer storm: the hail in bucket-loads
piled up against the verges of the roads,
the wind shrieking like a song
sung wrong,
the clouds come down darker still
beyond the hill,
and children dancing in the rain, stripped bare
as unabashed as wildwood deer.

A gawky girl is prancing there
who knows the world may watch but doesn't care,
a boy who's keen on bees and bugs
and slugs
is taking stiff-legged steps to show
how beetles go –
and here's the youngest, little one
who merely wants to jump and run.

And gone like that: storm and childhood too,
the hailstones into mud, the sky back blue,
the garden flowers standing tall
and all
the children bathed and in their beds,
their fragrant heads
filled full with how by chance
a sudden rainstorm made them dance.

Seasonal Variations on a Double Theme

for Chris Saunders and Michele de Kretser

SPRING

The sparrows in our hedgerow are arguing
So fiercely they hardly notice a stranger
Who now comes sauntering into their airspace.
It's possible, says the postman, that at last
Spring may be considering an arrival.
He hoicks his bag on his back and refuses
A second cup of coffee. The round beckons,
He says with his usual, never-hurried smile.
Primroses signify tacit agreement
And the celandine seem inclined to assent.
The sparrows resume their argumentation;
They have entirely forgotten to beware
The sparrowhawk's sudden entry, from stage left.

Of such things we are required to take account.
This is a peaceful world of postmen calling
But ill tidings come bound in the same bundle
And the neighbour's angry posturing demands
Attention. He is disputing boundaries.
Such a silence pervades throughout the garden
When the sparrowhawk leaves, mission accomplished,
That what I know I know is more than enough.

SUMMER

High summer. Heat haze. Too hot to consider
Anything but shade. Walk the far side of streets
Out of the sun's blaze. Salt of sweat burns the eyes.
Bees have been banished, grass is burnished, brambles
Catch bare legs, make them bleed. The singular pink
Of guelder roses orchestrates the margins
Of bridleway and footpath. Cow parsley thickens.
Our neighbour's wife has found an old parasol
And parades it in her garden, wearing shorts.
"What the fock you starin' at?" her husband shouts,
Waving his spade as if it were a weapon.
Even the robin has retreated; he shelters
In the shadows lurking behind the pump house.

The relief of summer is in the thunder
As clouds form their strange shapes on the horizon.
Look, thunder says, growling at first, then in tones
That brook no opposing, Think you've got it made?
Not likely, even if I disperse myself;
You'd better be aware of my existence:
I'm the messenger, and my message is the storm:
What you know you know, but it's never enough.

AUTUMN

By small steps are big decisions made. The oaks
Are always the last to lose their leaves. I miss
The vivid red and orange of the maples
But pastel shades of English brown and yellow
Soothe and soften. This is a gentle country,
I am inclined to think, as I stroll its paths.
That's till the bellicose neighbour berates me
Because (he says) I walked near his house last night;
He'll do me in for trespass. Back off, my friend,
This is bountiful autumn: enough for you,
Enough for almost everyone. But he doesn't agree.
The beech-leaves have turned; the ash is turning, too,
But I'm inclined to stand my limited ground.

Sometimes mere ineptitude provokes conflict;
Polite words, gestures, demurral, forbearance,
An exercise of practised diplomacy:
I am proffered good advice by those who know
Much more than I do. I wish to be peaceful,
To match the season; but how far, my judges,
How far? When does compromise turn cowardly?
What I know I knew, I fear I'm forgetting.

WINTER

So: to winter, hurtling in on northeast winds,
Prising paint off the weatherboarding. Try this
For size, the raindrops proclaim as their muscles
Swell to icicles. Look, we can loosen even the cobbles.
The leaves of the lilies crumple, the mortar
In the brickwork crumbles, the cast iron rusts.
It seems our neighbour has upped and off somewhere;
The debt-collector's van is almost blocking the lane.
The postman says he will miss the excitement
Of smiling at a raging recipient,
But bundles himself quickly back in his van.
Our boundaries are safe from imprecations
And incursions, but winter thinks otherwise.

You weep? No, it's just an old man's rheumy eyes.
It means nothing, this crying. I do not mourn
My own decrepitude, nor the death of friends.
If I wept, it'd be at what's impossible:
To have chosen to live my life differently,
To believe what I don't credit. I repent
Of far too much, but I forgive too little.
What I thought I knew, I fear I've forgotten.

Diary Entry

I'm more than half-asleep, and in a vein
a cannula. To this will be attached
quite soon a tube, and into it will pour
sedation and some other stuff.
There is a minor chance, the surgeon said,
of something going wrong. How will I know?
I asked. I think he smiled. It's strange once more
to feel a little like a child, not scared
but hardly in control of destiny
or even destination.
"Will this be over soon?"
or "Are we nearly there?"

I'm asked if I would like
some music on. Mozart, I plead,
but what we get is something else
which sounds as if it's from a funeral march.
Please turn that off, the surgeon says: no dirges now...
And then I must have drifted off.
I don't know where I went inside my head.
Is 'drift' the word I want? It wasn't 'drown'.
I went alone, I think. Familiar sounds
and lots of space, like walking on a beach.
And nothing much to care about,
and nothing owed. No "obligation".
And some time later I returned.
One has to wait for things to settle down.
I guess this won't be over soon,
but maybe we are nearly there.

Consolation

"Tell me how old I am."
– ELIZABETH BISHOP, 'The Mountain'

Once, I made a child believe
since size it is that measures years
(so true, when five outstrips three by far)
that I, at six foot four,
was older than the oldest there
by multiples not guessed at.

And then, before the year was out,
that same kind child turned to me,
consoled me in decrepitude:
"I'm sorry that you're old," she said.
"It doesn't matter, we don't mind –
and you won't know when you're dead."

Fragment

Sun, then shadows spiralling
across the lawn and into the poppies
as if released by what is barely wind.
Things you said I find I half-remember
but didn't take the time to note.
Who cares?
I have a small desire to know better
what I should have recorded.
My turn it is to mow the lawn.
You will sit in a deckchair to watch me.

In a French Garden

The sparrowhawk that rules this tract of land
between the barn and walnut trees
has found a vantage place.
From there, it tells the truth about its world:
death is absolute.

Below the unpruned apple grove
a tribe of hoopoes scratch and search,
panaches furled, then flared:
abundant life, it seems to me.

Old Oak

Our neighbour trimmed the worst of it last year
in hope he wouldn't need to do much more;
but now he's had the oak cut down, right down.
The reasons that he gave made sense, I guess,
for not so long ago a half-dead branch
brought down his power lines – and ours as well –
but still it might have stood for thirty years,
which would have been enough for us, for sure.
Since life's abundant even in decay,
sustaining what's not easily observed,
the jackdaws nested there, woodpeckers too,
adorned in black and scarlet finery,
and celebrating with a rat-tat-tat
of drums...now all have gone away, away,
the smaller branches burned, the trunk chopped up
for fuel, and who knows where the birds have gone?
It's rotten to the core, the woodman said,
although the V his screaming chainsaw cut
showed wood that looked to us as good as new.
Still, down it came, with heartfelt groans attendant
on its fall. Or was that me? The woodman waits.

An All-Night Lullaby

Sleep sound, my dearest one, sleep sound:
the noisy world goes whizzing round
and you are head-down deep in sleep
and deep in sleep may you still stay
while light slides on to the edge of day.

At dawn, the birds begin their song:
the blackbird, thrush and chaffinch too,
sing How d'you do, you two, you two,
and still you sleep the whole night through,
however loud or long that song.

And so I drag myself awake
to murmur gently, "For your sake"
and was that really all the night
        (all night, all right)
so interrupted by the sun?
And still you sleep, my dearest one.

Poem for the One Only

As we walk, she says she hears
waxwing, fieldfare and redwing;
you never see them now, she says,
but, if you listen, you can hear them sing.

Above, the clouds accumulate
to what may yet become a storm.
The brambles stretch across the path
to slow us down.

We're coming closer every day
to where things end, that gulping beast
that swallows everyone
as if we didn't matter in the least.

And who'll go first, you or me?
Me, who worries if you go alone
to town? You, afraid I might indulge
(old fool) in this or that, too much, too soon?

Think of something else, you say, something nice.
The oaks have held their leaves
later than the ash, though colours merge –
and somewhere far away a raptor grieves.

Words & Music
for the Romney Marshes

SPOKEN INTRODUCTION

Tempting, is it not, to think that the best answers
are always the most simple. Thus, we might like
to suppose words mean and music doesn't,
not exactly by the same measure words do,
as orders handed out, directions given.
No one obeys music, as we obey words,
no one listens to a sonata as if it were
the voice of a satnav. But think now of poems,
which are made out of words but are more than that,
as music is made of sounds but silence too –
and he who cannot dance must walk, stately steps
as if the music started there, a minuet
or sarabande, courante or gigue. The poem too
cannot help but dance; it's there in the rhythm
of the words, as in the way the heart must beat.
So we might claim that poems are really music
or that music is in a way poetry –
but that would be over-simplification,
which we've had enough of from politicians
and compilers of protocols. What we want
is complication, to hope that the array
of human awkwardness should be acknowledged.
We are dealing here with meaning, but also
with uncertainty, and blurring of edges,
knowing that the same music that may fill me
with sadness makes the one next to me joyful.

Poems aren't feeling, any more than music is;
both may make you weep, or reach for the off-switch:
or you could, if you're not enjoying yourself,
get up noisily – or politely – and leave.
Who is it steals meaning from experience?
Maybe it's only those who require answers
to everything, who can't be content with silence.
Landscape cannot be abstracted from water,
or at least the effects of water, or else
the lack of it. So, these marshes were once sea,
and these words may somehow have music added.
So, the imagination shifts and alters
as it struggles to come to terms with itself,
to make some sort of sense out of words and music,
silences between the words, between the notes,
after the words, and after the music ends.

LYRIC
(for a single voice plus instrument)

Entangled with this voice
let the single fiddle sound,
interweaving like a rope
   despair and hope:

a strand, a turn, a bend,
a twist and (listen) last
a tug to tighten fast
   despair and hope.

Despair sans counterpart –
like crying in the light –
soon frays and pulls apart
   and breaks your heart,

and hope without despair
is shouting in the dark
that we can see all right
   despite the night –

and thus, the voice and verse,
entwined as twins, first wind
and then unwind the two,
   as echoes do
       (as echoes do)...

CHORUS

Sing we our songs of the Romney marshlands,
compost & leaf mould, silt, shingle & sand,
on this level of earth, older than England,
reclaimed from the sea by work of the hands:

Over the marshes the breeze sidles sideways,
idles in eddies, then suddenly lifts,
dances like shadows in gossamer shifts
where sunlight lances the afternoon haze.

Swallows are wheeling over the wetland
patterning clouds. Sheep are sauntering slow
to their pasture, fleeces like clouds down low:
compost & leaf-mould, silt, shingle & sand.

Down from the Denge to old Dungeness side
run ditches and dykes to the cold North Sea;
on innings of Dymchurch, sewers of Rhee,
sluice-gates are lowered to hold back the tide.

Brenzett & Burwash, Camber & Brookland,
St Mary the Virgin deep in the Marsh,
Littlestone, Greatstone, remains of the Marsh:
compost & leaf mould, silt, shingle & sand...

L'ENVOI
(duet with single instrument)

What was water now is land
   yet may one day be
         returned to sea.

Voices too are silent now,
   all dispersed in air:
         or can you hear

still in the afternoon sun
   the echoes of song
         shadowing long?

Nietgenaamd

for Gus Ferguson

A signpost in the veld
directs you off your route
to Nietgenaamd: somewhere
that's not without a name
but named without a name.

And so you'd find yourself
lost perhaps, looking still:
was it that place we passed
an hour or two ago?
Perhaps we missed the sign.

And is it far to go
to get to Nietgenaamd?
As friends forget our names,
as words escape our brains?
My home's in Nietgenaamd.
I've lived there all my life.

Omdraaivlei

So when we reached this spot, we knew we'd come
too far. We turned our transport round again
and gave the place its name. We could've called it
something else: Retreat, perhaps. Defeat? Too Far?

There were no mountains, no ravines: a plain
that stretched ahead for miles and miles and miles,
no streams, no lakes, nor even sour bush,
just open veld. The roads will not be made.

Where blood and bullets once prevailed, our will
to fight another war has died. We've learned
to fear the traps, the branches on the road,
the pits with poisoned spikes, the secret bombs

which blow your legs away. You look behind
and someone's closed the road; you turn again
and now you see the barricades ahead,
the cheerful soldiers in their armoured cars.

So don't delay to make this turnabout,
and since we've learned to make the language mean
the stuff we want, don't call it "turning back":
"Retrieve the high advance", let's call it that.

A counsel of despair? The loser lost?
The prize we looked for gone to someone else?
Don't care too much, my friend: the future waits.
Let us pretend the future always wins.

Droëwaterval

on the Swartberg Pass

Was it ever thus, the waterfall
Where water never fell?
Did we expect too much, who hoped
That all might share abundant gold?
The baby-faced assassin in a suit
Giggles on his throne;
The policemen wave aloft their whips.
Burn the books; they tell too many lies.
My ancient friends who manned the barricades
Must shrug their shoulders now;
They fear that what we won is lost again.
Who would have guessed that it might come to this?
Dit is wat dit is. It is what it is.

High Hurdles

i.m. Randolph Vigne

Since no one wants to win this race, it's best
To saunter in towards the end, to post
A message to your friends, to mouth a jest,
High-five the man who stopped the clock, almost
As if you'd made a choice. Should we deplore
We're heading west? Or else negotiate
A secret deal by which we offer more
Than sparse remains to nourish God's estate?
The books have all been burned or banned, the map
Re-drawn, the times turned upside down, the hell
We lived in once called something else. It's past,
Old friend, the double-clanking call, the bell
That tells us all: this is the final lap –
And still the highest hurdle is the last.

Verkeerdekraal

"We have erred and strayed from Thy ways like lost sheep."
– The Book of Common Prayer

So did we get it wrong, those years ago?
That's 'we', the brainy boys and girls, elite
And blessed in every sort of way, judgmental
To a fault, agnostic to be sure.

We thought we knew exactly who we were.
We chose precisely who to kill with what;
The damage that we can't undo we call
'collateral' – we know we can't be blamed.

And now, like sheep who've nudged a broken hedge
Aside, we claim we did our best to learn
The lessons of duality. Our wars
Were 'little wars' and made to keep the peace.

So, turn the wagons round and head for home,
Though home might never be the place it was;
The roadblocks lie ahead; the policemen pounce
On penitents and pilgrims all alike

And here's their list of those to be detained –
Although there's nothing left which points to guilt:
The blood was washed away, the bodies burned,
The clothes we wore all parcelled up and dumped.

I told you, sir, as clearly as I could
I must have dropped my weapon in a ditch.
We built our lives on emptiness, and found
No solace when – at last – time caught us out.

A Sort of Prayer

for JM Coetzee

> *"...for to love and live beloved is the soule's paradise*
> *both here and in heaven."*
> – *JOHN WINTHROP*, A Modell of Christian Charity

To whom then might I pray, as we get old
and older still, before the mason carves
the final date on the memorial stone?
Or should I cry, Enough, enough, old friend,
let me alone once more that I may flaunt
those strange devices of my crooked heart
with no one there to tell me what 'they' thought
I thought or what 'they' thought I should have thought
if only I had been as wise as 'them'.

Right now, on my last day in Africa,
I'm on a flight to the Golden City –
Egoli, as it used to be, though now
I find I'm losing that old track of names
not only since they changed or doubled up.
Let's call the past a sort of catapult
that weakened wrists can hardly pull.
The stone's no arrow now. It merely falls
the little way between the pull and splash.

Why then might anyone but us assume
that fluttering at the window is a ghost
who tries to get inside (or is it out)?

Is it surprising then to find at last
that we might want to live our final days
in multiples of ambiguity?

I nearly killed you once, not long ago:
I fell asleep driving in the deep Karoo
and crashed the hire car into a ditch.
I heard you shout my name as I heaved the wheel
too late to miss the scrub, the fence, the trees.

Should I address this prayer to you, old friend,
or to the steadfast one we both have loved
(in our different ways) for much longer now
than we once hoped we would survive?
We lean on love as we falter to the stairs,
and hope for someone strong to cushion us
when (it's bound to happen) we trip and fall.

And so I pay, with scant humility,
this episodic homage to our past.
Who would have guessed, when we were young, the way
the world turned out to be: to change so fast,
yet stay the same, to shift, to sink, to drown?
No one would ever call it simple now.
Was it not more than all we might have hoped
for you, for me, although in different ways?
What fortunes were they that we didn't earn?
Contentment not the aim, but all the same
to love and know for sure that one is loved.

In the Water-Margins

Here, at the water's edge, in a cabin on stilts,
I am listening to what the reeds are telling me
in a kind of breathless whispering, *as if... as if... as if...*
So indefinite that the words are like swallows flittering low
but too fast to be caught by anyone or anything
except as streaks on the edge of one's retina
like smears of ink on a faded Chinese manuscript...

And then, in your most matter-of-fact voice, you say
It's just the noise of the wind in the reeds and the water moving
when the reeds are shuffled backwards and forwards.
So, you scoff at me like a postmodernist philosopher:
Do you really think you can hear what the reeds say?
You may as well try to catch the swallows as they curve
down to the meniscus of the water and then upwards.

The water-margins are where troublemakers were sent
by the emperor and his mandarins when they'd had enough
of their insidious garrulity, inconstancy, duplicity.
Even here at home, even in what was once my own country,
the soul gets sent away, out of all imagining.
What the reeds are saying as the wind passes between them
are aspirant conditionals, *as if*, *if only*, and *provided*.

As if everything, that's what the reed bed is saying,
which isn't much different from *as if nothing*,
when nothing and victory may be synonymous.
It's no good you telling me it should be otherwise;
if you can't hear what I hear when the reeds gossip to me,
it's because you seem to know precisely that this is personal;
you suppose the noise is sans significance, the words without meaning.

Even when you think there is nothing that matters,
something does. And that turns out to be the biggest puzzle,
that there should be something at all, and not just nothing.
This is what I am having such trouble with, when I hear
that persistent chorus. I feared those voices would be baleful;
instead, they are kind of peaceful, kind of accepting,
maybe even kind of kindly, here in the water-margins.

On Shadows

for Ken Gross & Liza Lorwin

We learn to live with silence. Nothing new
obtrudes. There is an older peace
than we were told about, in which we learn
the impossibilities, like wishing things
had been a little different.
            Excuses multiply,
even when we've given up
on obligations. Accept the world
for what it is.
    The moon has shadows too.

Puppets
for Ken Gross

They mimic what we think
But have no thoughts,
And even out of sorts
   They never blink.

Flesh of wood, joints of tin,
Sinews strung from string:
Strangle them, stab or sting
   And still they grin.

They slather over sex
And smutty jokes,
But claim they're decent folks
   Who crane their necks.

They stagger and they reel,
They grab your sleeve,
They plead you must believe
   They never steal.

They specialize in lies
And subterfuge,
Pretending to be huge
   Monsters quarter-size.

Why pity those who cry
But cannot bleed?
They claim to know our need
    Before we sigh

And, when they're hung up high
Or dumped on shelves,
They stay their same old selves
    And never die.

Arm will argue with its wrist,
Thumb deny its hand.
Puppets say: We understand
    But mean: We jest.

Rhyming Runes for Magical Dan

i.m. Dan Wilson (1977–2016)

About the final letting go
we can't pretend to know.

Things pile up, unwittingly:
obligations, fittingly,

Interpretations, accents, words,
like beasts corralled in herds.

We thought we'd seen the worst;
who guessed the worst comes first?

No one queues at heaven's gate;
no one says, "You've come too late."

The hope for grace hereafter
you learned from children's laughter.

The Lesson

I thought I'd learned to watch
my every stumbling step
(look down, look up) –
it's guesswork which is which –

but then I looked away
and caught a glance of light –
so swift, so bright,
it almost seemed like day;

and who is there can tell
if it is worth the cost
of what gets lost?
Entranced, I tripped and fell.

Rhymes for an Old Friend in Trouble

We seldom get what we deserve:
luck, like light, travels in a curve.

Yet how we wish this were the norm:
to promise what we then perform.

The world's a complicated place,
where grief walks hand in hand with grace,

a paradigm of love unearned,
revenge reserved, reward returned,

a kind of chaos thickly sprayed
to thwart the best plans ever made

and all advice the old can give
subsumed in this: you learn to live.

Last Lesson of a Wintry Afternoon:
a Kaddish for Joanna, Lady Seldon

Have we lost you then, brightly coloured lass?
Our Perdita who won't come back again?
Perhaps the sideways light of wintry sun
may teach us how to cope with grief, to learn
acceptance of the things which can't be changed.
Is it so strange that we should turn to you
to ask for lessons in how best to mourn?
You always gave the news to us quite straight,
however bleak it seemed.
    "Do not pretend,"
you said: "I know what's coming next". And now
there is no next. The future has arrived.
"So gather round, my last timetabled class:
a lesson for a winter's afternoon..."
And thus instruction comes. Wear something bright:
a purple scarf. A crimson cap. A splash
of scarlet countermanding all this gloom.
And use the words we've known from ages past,
the psalms, the prayers, the chants. And tell the truth:
the books for children whom you will not know,
and poems, and prose (unedited, but done) –
so much undone, and yet so much was done.
You taught us how to look at death, and smile.

Telling the Truth

i.m. Edward Thomas

I walk the streets
Of what I once
Thought of as home.
It isn't now.

Old age retreats.
What happened since
Fell out of time:
I don't know how.

The past colludes
To make one say
That grace persists –
It never does.

As stone obtrudes
Through graded clay,
The real insists.
It always has.

What ends our song
Is never known:
The rifle shot
Right through the throat,

The pulse gone wrong,
The cancer grown.
What is, what's not,
Have found us out.

A Game of Tennis

Well, old man, it seems I've beaten you
by twenty years. And now I'm old myself
somehow this victory doesn't seem
to matter much.
It's not the tennis match we used to play
which laid a fiver on each set I won.
Indeed, I'd swap a win for just a day
to let you see my children, and their children too,
the multiplying generations
you didn't live to see.
No chance of that, I know,
although you thought you'd keep a loving eye
somehow on all that happened here below.
I doubt the hope of that
although it's hard to judge our souls are smashed
to smithereens of dust
and nothing left but words.
I count them out:
six-four, six-all, a set, the match.

The Short History of a War

At first it seemed a place where one might dream
of being at peace: a ring of sheltering hills;
old gardens full of apple trees; a stream
which sauntered down through dry-stone walls;

a poplar grove and flowering shrubs. We saw
where barns and houses might be built, a field
to fence for horses or for cows. The more
we looked, the more like home it seemed.

And then our guide, the farmer, said, "It's cursed,
this place. Those whitewashed stones? They're graves. And more
up there, on top. And those were not the worst
we found. We don't forget the war,

not here. The children's bodies in a pit –
the mothers found them there. Why kill the kids?
The girls and babies too. Their throats were slit.
And that's not what they did to lads."

We picked our way up past the rocks, and heard
his story panted out in bursts: the war
which tore the land in bits; no place to hide;
no way to tell whom you should fear

when neighbours might be worst of all. Too late
to make amends; we'd rather shoot the lot
and bury grief. And so put out the light,
compound for good the ancestral debt.

From higher up we see, in shades of green,
where homesteads must have stood, and guess the shape
of all the lives which flourished here, a plan
that someone scrawled across: no hope.

"No building here," the farmer tells his guests.
"I know which side I'm on, but never say:
I'll deal with snakes and graves, but not with ghosts."
What else to do but look away?

And who remembers now what was the cause?
We've learned too well how wars are lost and won;
nor does it matter when this history was.
It happened once. It will again.

Paradigm

Having dispensed
with obligation,
his mind shut tight
against abstraction,

what he wants these days
is something simple,
nearing the end,
an example.

Instead, what he's getting
is otherwise:
complication
and yet more lies.

And so he falters
as stairs get steeper
and can't accept
what he can't alter.

For My Dead Brother
after Catullus 101

So many years, and countries too:
I thought I'd said farewell to you.

This little gift can't do much good
(I'd hand it over if it would)

but there aren't even ashes left,
just dirt and dust – and me, bereft.

How different now our lives might be
if you had lived as long as me.

I face the fact: I too must die
so greet you now: my last goodbye.

End-Rhymes

Since this may be my final song,
it won't be loud and won't be long.

Heroic past went sauntering by,
and doffed his hat to say goodbye.

I started somewhere else, then grew
into a person strange and new –

and now, however I am seen,
I'm not the man I might have been.

The closer still I get, the less
I care to know, the more I guess.

Who knows what shape our lives will take?
I'll go to sleep and will not wake.

I'd like to claim I made a choice:
rejoice, again I say, rejoice.

An Old Man & His Wife

He saw a butterfly, half-drowned,
and swam to rescue it; a palm
then spilled it on the pool's surround:
a pretty fragment saved from harm.

He knew that sun dries butterflies
but, later, walking where it lay,
he found, with something like surprise,
it had already flown away.

"And if you'd found a wasp, half-dead,
that swam in frantic circles there,
would you have saved that too?" she said.
And, yes, he would, despite his fear.

You cannot have the one, and not
the rest: the hapless butterfly,
the dangerous wasp. Like love, the lot
comes undivided: smile, and sigh.

Poems from the Chinese

The ways of the world grow more mysterious.
I am no longer sure I know even where my home is.
All the same, I pluck four acorns from an oak tree as I am passing
and hand them to a grandchild as a greeting.

I wish I had learned more from experience.
Now I am old I am appalled by my ignorance.
But this evening we sat in the twilight waiting to hear if the owl called
and were undeterred by its silence.

Is it true that parents love their children more than their children
    love them?
Our arrival is ignored because they are reading
but later, when I am dozing after dinner,
a granddaughter kisses the top of my head.

Most days, I wake before dawn.
Nothing else moves in the household,
although a jay is arguing about something in the woods above us.
I walk in the garden, noting dewdrops on the petals.

Mainly, I think of time as my master
and I a poor mandarin to serve it;
then, without warning, there are moments
when I am a dam wall holding back a river in flood.

Sometimes you scare me, old friend, with your certainties.
Is doubt so perilous?
Exploring a landscape, we negotiate overgrown footpaths
but seem to end at much the same destination.

The grey heron that fishes on the far bank of the river
has advised me (not in words) that I shall live
a good many years longer still. Should I be grateful?
He gathers his wings and moves himself to somewhere further up the river.

Time was, I knew my place in the ways of living, as things are ordered;
older now, I've forgotten:
still, I notice, when I walk the fields beyond the palace,
the sentries don't bother to challenge me.

In the ploughed lands beyond the ditches I count four egrets and a heron.
The paleness of egrets makes them easy to see:
not so the heron, even when there's only one.
Yet he is fearful and flies away from my staring.

Easiest of all would be always to do the opposite of what is expected;
intention is never in doubt then.
In the same way, the raptor stays in the desolate tree
even when the hunter with the shotgun approaches.

Back in the city, I imagine the countryside once more:
an avenue of plane trees,
a surfeit of pigeons,
and the Council has forgotten to prune the municipal roses.

Walking to the Paradise Gardens

i.m. Griffiths and Victoria Mxenge

> "No government can forgive.
> No commission can forgive.
> Only I can forgive. And I'm not ready yet."
> – A witness at the TRC

> "You let men ride over our heads
> We went through fire and water
> But you brought us out into a place of liberty."
> – Psalm 66.11

Why stand we then in such jeopardy
every hour of every waking day,
worse on those nights when intruders come
crowding once again into our cells,
grinning behind their masks, grimacing,
shaking us from sleep? I tell you:
this was no black man; I could see
white skin between his gloves and the sleeves.
But the sergeant who caught me said, No,
this was our people, gangsters, bandits;
but I could see, I could see...

Like throwing stones at the wind...

Laughing, my tall friend in the front row –
at Fort Hare in Alice where the main game
was debating, though with a sharp edge
since the wrong words could send you to gaol
or exile – signalled me to beware
that the question came from an informer
	(agent provocateur at the least...)

And then for a time Robben Island –
that other great university –
afterwards, making trouble in the courts,
just one step ahead, using the tricks,
slipping down the alleys and byways,
playing the law like the lawyer he was.

They were waiting for him at the crossroads,
in a big car, black, a Ford, he thought;
they had torches, four or five of them,
and waved him down, and he thought maybe
there'd been an accident, a roadblock.
He should have swerved then, or gone faster,
but they would have caught him anyway.
They had done with talking now, he saw.

First our friends were murdered, then their wives,
then the witnesses sent out of town –
somewhere, anywhere, who knows, who cares?
The point is that no one comes to judgement;
and if (since?) there is no God nor will they.

So many people, so many deaths:
and it shouldn't be just those we know
who matter; but it is our nature
(I guess) to care for those close to home.
What good does it do, telling the tale
over and over again? Books get burned,
words unlearned, the beggars coming to town.
I will tell you the story again, again.

Because that's the way the world was made:
the lawyer come to such a lawless end –
but he fought back, using the knife he pulled
from his own chest, until someone slugged him
from behind. No passive victim this,
no acquiescence as the files trudged
through the deep forests, with the guards
only at distant ends. This one fought.

And he lost, one against four or five:
the white man and three or four hirelings,
careless of death as the Gestapo.
Hacked, disembowelled, ears sliced off almost,
disfigured – his blood made dirt of dust.

The lawyer's wife too, because she
would not keep her mouth shut, jabber, jabber:
I mean, we warned her, didn't we, often enough?
Then we – in our turn – shut it for her.
And the horror of that execution
(Do you really want to hear the details?)
in a dark hut, with the children nearby,

and you may as well do the job properly
as the English say, penny and pound,
or is it eggs broken for the omelette,
or some image far, far worse than that?
What kind of man would shoot a child asleep,
wrapped against the cruel cold in blankets?
It was Dirk Coetzee who cut my throat...

And still, when I fall asleep, there comes
such knocking at the door I must wake –
and there's no one there; but he comes back
knocking, knocking, though I've barred the door.

    Have we grown so far beyond judgement?
    Have we learned anything? Have we taught
    our neighbours? Much less our enemies?
    How little I know now – except for this:
    what is done is done and, if they see still,
    they will sing for their children, and cheer
    loudly with their friends and their comrades.
    Sacrifice doesn't need to make sense,
    doesn't need a future. It is done
    because without hope there's no point, no point
    at all. We must all stand up sometimes.

    I walk now, with sun on my face, to the uplands:
    I am walking through the azaleas
    of Kirstenbosch as the low clouds lift.
    I am walking on the pine-needle paths
    of the mountain contours above Tokai,
    up the stone-clad hillsides to the orchards

of Pomerol, as bountiful as autumn.
I'm walking to the paradise gardens
high in the mountains above Shalimar
beyond even the Gardens of Babylon.
Down in the valley there is Lake Nageen
where the houseboats are moored at the jetties,
and the flower sellers are drifting home.

Song of the Sparrows

in the plague year, 2020

"But for a time...
they were almost as free as the sparrows..."
– WILLIAM MAXWELL, Time Will Darken It

The sparrows in our garden
have freedoms we've mislaid;
they come and go – chattering –
as if they aren't afraid;

until (of course) the sparrowhawk
invades their springtime busy-ness.
A silence flowers then, assures
the balancing of more with less.

I turn to you, as always, love,
who feeds the birds and knows each name;
we're both aware what waits for us
but tend the garden, just the same.

Breathless

a meditation

I'm told it's like an illness to be thus
obsessed with words and what they mean, as if
by getting down precisely what I thought
I meant (although I didn't know I'd meant it
until I got it down) would help me catch
that fleeting world outside, the sudden noise
the pigeons make, flapping from the edge
of water trough to where the wires stretch

above the hedge, dividing up the sky
in cubist bits, until the spiralled flight
of cabbage white, the splash incarnadine
where unpruned roses found a way to climb
upward through the apple tree, the beech leaves
autumnal early, muddled up that plan –
no pattern pre-ordained survives at all
since nothing's settled here. Oh, breathless, breathless…

Insubstantial stuff the flesh turned out to be
though I was warned. I thought this can't be me,
it must be someone else, a nicer bloke,
good-tempered too, a patient chap, and kind,
inclined to see the best in everyone
and never swift to judge. And so: ho ho,
but better that than my old mate, despair,
who taunts me when I want to hesitate.

The world is never still; you'd think it might
at least slow down a tad to let us catch
its twists and turns, its spinning round, but No:
it races on and on, sprinting for the tape,
as breathless as an old man climbing up
the steeper second flight of stairs to bed,
which may or may not let him sleep all night
until he gets to what he hopes is dawn.

A Letter to Maeder Osler on My 70ᵗʰ Birthday

"Im Kampf zwischen Dir und der Welt, sekondiere der Welt."
– *FRANZ KAFKA*, Die Zürauer Aphorismen

Old friend, a continent away,
imagine now (if – please – you will)
one single thing that might be changed
in all these years we've been alive;
it's not that consequence entails,
but precedence ensures. Take fame:
we tried it once, when we were young,
and found we didn't like it much;
we ran away from every chance,
so should we now relive that choice?
or emulate those clever friends,
who win the prizes every time?
As if we could, by wishing so –
yet wouldn't swap our lives for theirs,
not I for yours, nor you for mine.
    No way!
And now we know the things we do
would we undo that loss of love
that cut us down as if we were …
(say) trees? All that upstanding pride!
The shade we cast! The roots spread wide
to bear the wild wind's fiercest force!
False epithets, false rhyme, full fall.

Turned out to my surprise – and yours –
we went on growing much the same
(as trees will, even fallen down):
we found capacious lives, new homes,
careers, a niche, a kind of name;
too much undone, of course, but still
we'd have to say it was success...

So: time to reckon up the score
of you and me against the world
we didn't change that much at all:
nil-nil? A goal or two apiece?
Or did it win on penalties?
We didn't always do the things
we thought we might; but should we be
content enough? I'm not. Are you?
I know it seems a little mean
to undervalue such rewards.
They're rich enough, for both of us.
But guilt? Oh, that comes flooding in
like droves of sheep that edge and nudge

their way through gaps you'd hardly think
were there at all. Can one expunge
the dirty bits? Those slimy lies
that didn't need be told at all?
Or does one simply shrug and say:
there's little point in looking back?
Oh, well: my birthday's almost gone
and I'm three score years and ten.
You've got that coming soon, old friend:

the years behind a broken trail
of arrows, footprints, love and loss,
the years ahead a steeper climb.
Advice? I wouldn't dare. I've leaned
much more on you than you on me.
I crossed the bleak bits out of this
memorandum on getting old;
you wouldn't let self-pity join
our party as a welcome guest.
We've learned we have to wait – and wait –
for maybe there is still surprise
in store – and it might even be
in time. It can't be otherwise.

> *The shadows spiral on the wall*
> *of this small study where I write;*
> *refractions of the sunlight fall*
> *as planes of colour, tinged with white.*

> *The wind makes music in the pines*
> *and wisps of green are taking flight*
> *(*rallentando*) as evening spins*
> *its whirlpool way to deeper night.*

> *The darkness now seems darker still,*
> *and eddies down the edge of sight,*
> *goes twisting down and down, until*
> *it seems so deep it's almost light.*

Endpiece

Far gone? Gone for good? I abjure
All pre-knowledge, but now I know for sure.
You (the reader) don't; or do you?
I wrote this before I knew.

NOTES

p. 69, 'The Writing on the Wall':

> "Or open to winds and waves
> Ligurian cemeteries!
> A rosy sadness colours you
> When in the evening, similar to a flower
> That rotted, the great light
> Falls apart and dies."
>
> – from 'Liguria', by VINCENZO CARDARELLI,
> engraved on a wall of the public cemetery
> of Manarola in the Cinque Terre

p. 129, 'A Letter to Maeder Osler on My 70th Birthday':

> "In the struggle between yourself and the world, be the
> world's second."
>
> – from *Die Zürauer Aphorismen*
> (*The Zürau Aphorisms*), by FRANZ KAFKA

POETRY FOR THE PEOPLE

— RECENT RELEASES —

Jesus Thesis and Other Critical Fabulations by Kopano Maroga

An Illuminated Darkness by Jacques Coetzee

Rumblin' by Sihle Ntuli

Malibongwe: Poems from the Struggle by ANC Women edited by Sono Molefe

— RECENT AWARD-WINNING TITLES —

All the Places by Musawenkosi Khanyile
WINNER OF THE 2020 SOUTH AFRICAN LITERARY AWARD FOR POETRY
FINALIST FOR THE 2020 INGRID JONKER PRIZE

Zikr by Saaleha Idrees Bamjee
WINNER OF THE 2020 INGRID JONKER PRIZE

Everything is a Deathly Flower by Maneo Mohale
FINALIST FOR THE 2020 INGRID JONKER PRIZE

AVAILABLE FROM GOOD BOOKSTORES IN SOUTH AFRICA *&* NAMIBIA
& FROM THE AFRICAN BOOKS COLLECTIVE ELSEWHERE

UHLANGAPRESS.CO.ZA

Printed in the United States
by Baker & Taylor Publisher Services